My Alabaster Box

Katie McKee

BookLeaf Publishing

India | USA | UK

Presentation by *BookLeaf Publishing*

Web: www.bookleafpub.com

E-mail: info@bookleafpub.com

ISBN: 9789357615433

First edition 2023

I would like to dedicate this book to Kerri Nutbrown for all of the poems you read, the Friday afternoon assignments you gave, and the passion you ignited in me. Thank you for believing in me more than I could have ever believed in myself.

This is for you.

ACKNOWLEDGEMENT

I would like to acknowledge everyone who has supported my writing over the years. Specifically, my family for always allowing me to follow my dreams and providing me with endless opportunities.

My English teachers for your dedication to the profession and constant feedback on how I could improve my writing abilities.

My Pastors for the guidance, support, prayers, and encouragement. I would like to especially acknowledge Pastor Jaunty for giving me the assignment to write a book and never doubting that it would become a reality.

All of my friends in CMFI, too many to count, who have encouraged me to continue writing. Thank you for your ongoing support, it means more than you could ever know.

Who I Am

I was that kid who wouldn't stop crying unless I
was in my mother's arms. I was that kid who wrote
on the walls with crayons. I was that kid that
looked so adorable on the outside but too smart
for her own good on the inside. I was that kid
who'd go to school with messy hair and dirt under
my nails. I was that kid who sat in the corner and
kept to herself. I was that kid lost in the shadow of
her twin. I was that kid who would fall over and
over again, but quickly say, "I'm okay" and stand
as if nothing had happened. But I was also the girl
determined to succeed, the one who agreed to
learn to read so that she could learn to write. I
quickly became the girl who could never sleep at
night and never wake in the morning. I was the kid
with a sign of warning written on my agenda for
my teachers to see. Soon after, I became the kid
who was always angry without cause. I was also
the girl who felt so guilty for that anger that it
consumed her. Completely. But then a shift
occurred as she discreetly concealed the pain she
had never healed from when she was younger.

Then I was the perfect daughter. Good grades. Good manners. Good shape. Good person. Good friend. Good writer. Just good. If only I knew to be good to myself. Of course, this façade could only survive for so long until everything in her small world went wrong. I was that teenager who desperately wanted to know who she was or would become. I was that teenager who felt too numb to be this young. I was that teenager whose silence was deafening. My name was hardly worth mentioning. I was the teenager who locked herself in her room on a Friday night and poured out her cup of pain into poetry. I thought maybe then they'd notice me, but they didn't. I was the teenager who was closer to her teachers than her peers, whose soul seemed beyond the years of her body. I was the teenager who faded into the background and failed to be seen. I was mature, but naïve, or somewhere in between. I was the teenager who tried to commit suicide and failed. I always failed at the things I wanted most. I was the teenager in a psych ward at Christmas, a day of joy, just another patient hidden behind a veil of despair that would ware into the very flesh I tried to destroy. I was the teenager whose body was the host of a medicated concoction, like an auction of broken toys that little girls stopped using years ago.

I remember looking out of the hospital window
thinking of the world outside that place, but then I
caught a glimpse of my reflection in the mirror
and I swear I couldn't recognize my face. I'm the
young adult plagued by these memories, viewing
them as if they were yesterday. I'm the young
adult that still asks myself if I'm strong enough to
stay. I'm a young adult with honors in university,

surrounded by people who honestly love me. I'm
the young adult who turned her pain into passion,
and her passion into purpose. I'm the young adult
who prays to God each day, thanking Him for the
life that I've been given. I'm the young adult that
appears to be in the perfect position to heal. To

grow. To know who she is and who she'd become. I'm the girl who doesn't want to run away anymore, to close each door that opens simply because she doesn't know how to turn on the light, and she still can't sleep at night because she's afraid of the dark. Each time she allows it to surround her, it leaves another mark, another scar, to show her that she hasn't gone that far from that little girl drowning in her own tears, the one who added a new fear each year that she surpassed, they tell her not to live in the past, not to go back, but to keep her eyes ahead, but she's bleeding, and the only way to save her life is to find the place that bled with such abundance, excuse my redundancy.

But you need to pay attention and listen closely if you are to hear the screams of that little girl as she cries all alone in the bathroom with the water running faster than she ever could, It wasn't until the present day that I finally understood…I am perfection, and I'm also flawed, I speak my truth but I show my façade, I am joy, and I am sorrow, somehow I can live in yesterday and tomorrow, I am afraid, I am brave, as beautiful as life and as a hollow as a grave, I am good and I am fine, sometimes those words are difficult to define, I am that little girl and I am an adult, I used to be a variable but now I'm a result, and I can conclude that there is still more work to be done.

Note To Self

I was told to keep a picture of you close by. A reminder of your presence. A reminder that you are still with me and not only remain as a memory. But if I'm being honest, I'm afraid to look you in the eyes because then I'd have to admit that I let you down. That in the midst of the chaos, I lost sight of you for a time. All I could see was the smoke and I let go of your hand. I'm afraid that you wouldn't understand why it's taken me so long to come looking for you. If only you knew how long I've been looking in the wrong places, how many spaces I've had to occupy to try and find a location that never existed. How many nights I spent awake trying to run from the ache living in my heart. How many tears I lost thinking of you and what you'd be thinking of me. How many scars I placed on your skin, not realizing that our bodies were one. Not realizing that I was not the target of my inner criticism, you were. It was always directed at you. A baptism of suffering without justification, my fixation on perfection. An image that could only be created in my mind, unable to be replicated. Everything is calculated, but everything is complicated.

I've concentrated on protecting you only to see the limitations of your guard. Now you can't discard the lies you've been sold, and it's all because of the stories I've told as I tucked you into bed, the monster was never in your closet, it dwelled inside of your head. It preyed on you as you prayed to God back when you'd bow your knees on the floor each night hoping that you'd turn out alright. Before you close your eyes, why don't you take a long look? Do you like what you see? Are you proud of me? Mom, don't close the door just yet. Don't turn off the lights. I'm afraid of the dark. Remember when you used to be afraid of the dark? Back before it became your best friend. The only one on which you could depend. But, I'm here now, so you don't have to be afraid anymore. Is this version of me what you asked for? I'm trying to be the person you deserved many years ago. I know it's over, but is it too late? I've only shown you hate, but now I want you to teach me what it's like to love. What it's like to forgive. What it's like to be happy. Remember when you used to be happy? Me neither. I've been thinking about you a lot lately. Your smile. Your curiosity. Your kindness. And generosity. Then I think about the day it was all taken away. Of course, I can't remember the exact date or the circumstances that surrounded you. But I remember the pain when a piece of you broke.

I remember the weight of the first brick that
began the foundation of the walls you built. I
remember how it felt to watch joy slowly fade
away and not being able to reach it. I remember
the sound of your screaming that nobody else
could hear. The loneliness. The hopelessness. The
despair. As though nobody would care if you
disappeared too. As though nobody would even
notice. The truth is, there are so many people who
love you. So many people who only want to help
you. But you won't let them in, not after what I've
done to you. I'm sorry. I don't know if I ever told
you that before. I'm sorry for leaving you back
there. I'm sorry that nobody taught you to repair
the broken pieces of your mind. I'm sorry for the
contract I signed that gave away my rights to you.
I'm sorry for not staying by your side. I'm sorry
that all I've given you is blame. I'm sorry for the
shame and the guilt, for the choices I made on
your behalf. I'm sorry that all I have left of you is
this photograph. I'm sorry for allowing you to walk
into the arms of those boys. I'm sorry for the
constant noise, I'm just thinking out loud. I'm sorry
for how I've shaped the world in which you live and
I'm sorry for the pity that I give. I'm sorry for
telling you just to live when a survival guide was
not what you needed most. I'm sorry that I wasn't
the person who could hold you close and make
you feel safe. Instead, I watched you gasping for
air.

I'm sorry for each time that I would compare you to somebody else. Somebody who couldn't possibly understand what it was like to walk in your shoes. Shoes that were too big for you. Shoes that you needed to grow into. I'm sorry for causing you to think that you deserve less, that your success is worth more than your peace. It's because of me that you don't know how to relax.

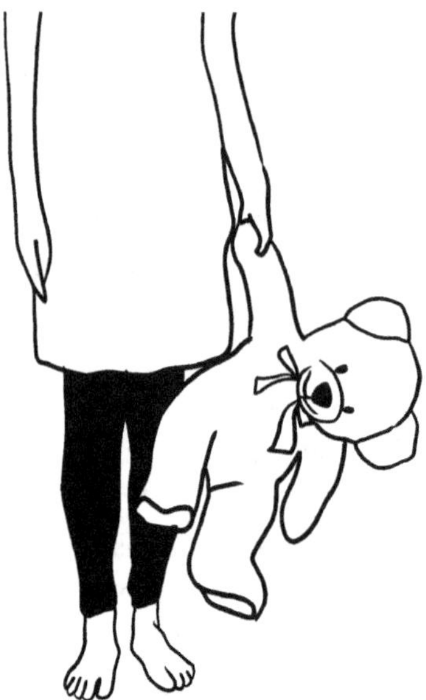

I'm sorry for pushing you into cracks because I was afraid to be vulnerable. Exposed. I'm sorry for each time I forced you to remain composed when you wanted so desperately to cry. To accept that what happened was not okay. I'm sorry for the way that I denied what you were feeling and told

you to move forward as though you'd lose your
place in the assembly line. I'm sorry for every time
you've said, "I'm fine", while fighting the truth on
the inside. I'm sorry for all of the compassion that
I couldn't provide. Not then and certainly not now.
Somehow my empathy only extends so far. Maybe
if you came closer, I could spare a kind word or
two. I'm sorry that you never knew how amazing
you were. How innocent. How pure. I'm sorry for
all that you've had to endure. Truly I am. But as I
stand here before you today with this note in my
hand, I need you to understand that none of this
was my fault and neither was it yours. You see,
locked doors don't give you the strength to open
windows and shadows don't exist without light.
You were a child, as was I.
Unassuming. Inexperienced. Vulnerable. In need of
constant care. Care that showed itself, but not in
the way that you needed. We needed. Generations
defeated in the eyes of one little girl, her whole
world depleted of its validity, too great rigidity and
not enough freedom. That's the thing about you
and me, and the whole idea of being free, we
would need to agree to rid ourselves of the debris
and simply be. Be who we were always meant to
be. Before the pain. Before the disappointment.
Before the regret. Before we were shaped into
someone we don't recognize anymore. Long
before you and I ever encountered one another.

Oh Mind, My Mind

Oh Mind, My mind! Our tangled tango is now
through
We have weathered the storms, your power only
grew
Darkness encompassed me while you watched and
glared
Was I a coward to admit that I was scared?

Your long fingers gripped the flesh around my
throat
Impaired by speech, you ignored the letter I wrote
I tried to plead and pray for a sign of your grace
In my search for mercy, I'd come to the wrong
place

My strength is withering with the wind as it blows
And the pain, Oh the pain no one even knows
Please let me tell one soul of my untimely demise
He laughed at me with a sense of surprise

"Do you really think that someone can hear you
cry
Go ahead scream, I dare you to try"

As he raised his toxic hands from my bruised skin
I was transported to somewhere I'd previously
been

Shouting to be free from the traumatic restraints
Feeling guilty for filing such uproarious complaints
What was I to do in a time of such great sorrow
Imagining a world where there is no tomorrow

While I fought to believe that mustn't be true
I witnessed optimism fade from my view
I refused to allow my mind to win this final round
But my ears could only hear one fatal sound

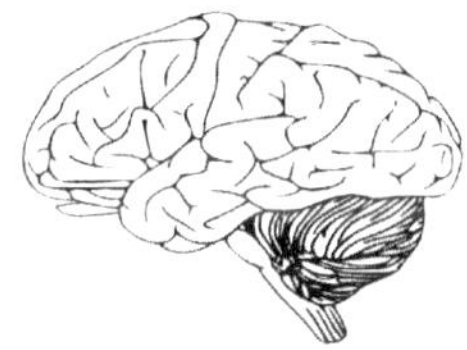

"Give up, give in, give me all that you have left
You may be okay now but your time will surely
come
I'll put you on trial for the actions of another
Until one day, you will be soul-stunningly numb
Unless you agree to grant custody of your mind
In that case, there's a bargain that you may find
I will control what you think, feel and be
But you my friend, you will be free… at last"

An inviting option for a soul I could not mend
I knew I didn't want this precious life to end
I had no idea that the finale was already here
As he quieted his voice to draw me near

"You are wiser than when you were young
Then, fear remained on the tip of your tongue
Don't worry, we still have lots of time to tell
On our path to the place, you know as hell"

I hope someone finds this before it's too late
Please hurry, for I don't have time to wait
Seconds wasted reading words on a page
I'm trapped with the one fuelled by rage

He is meticulous in manner and smart in spite
He lurks in the darkness produced by night
Feeds on the minds of the most pure from birth
And spreads his wickedness across the earth

Don't be fooled by his false promises and fable
Ignore the seduction intertwined with a label
Especially those who believe they are kind
Don't ever trust an overly involved mind

Oh mind, My mind, even when we're worlds apart
You speak to my soul and you break my heart

The Barrel

You were my second and final plan
Your bittersweet ending
Gave me hope
In some sort of strange way
You mesmerized me with the unknown
And spoke of endless possibilities
But something about you
Made me feel uneasy and nervous
Like you were almost too good
To be true, you know?
Like in a movie
When you think the ending
Is so obvious
But then it arrives
And it's not what you thought it would be
Maybe that's just life itself
Maybe nothing is for certain
Or maybe we have the control
After all it's our lives
It could just be me
But I believe
That if you stare motionless
Down the barrel of a gun
Long enough
Soon you will see yourself

Through that tiny hole
In which you rely
Every part of you in
Standing still
Shameful
Of what you want
But not brave enough
To do it.

The Monster

If I showed my true colors, what would society think?
Would they laugh, show pity or read the ink
I'm exhausted from smiling every single day
When I know the pain won't just go away
Every night I cannot sleep
Because my thoughts run so deep
They went out for a stroll
But got sucked into a black hole
My focus is no longer there; anywhere
I don't know why I'm like this I swear
It seems like I'm just well dressed
That just means how much I'm stressed
My friends all laugh and hang around
You don't need water to be drowned
This darkness beneath consumes my mind
It's like I'm living my life blind
On the outside I'm holding it together
But it's as unpredictable as the weather
"How are you" "I'm fine"
But the truth lies between the lines
It's like being on Mars and trying to breathe air
When they talk about the future, I don't really care

You say to suck it up and to be strong
But little do you know what exactly is wrong
My life is forever altered because of this
That cheerful 5-year-old is who I miss

This is war, you either win or die trying
You speak the truth or continue lying
The changes were all so very subtle I don't blame you
for not seeing
But what you don't understand is that I'm a human
being
The truth is you wouldn't last if this was in your brain
But I've found a way to numb the pain
I have to fight my mind every single second
But that's only because this thing had beckoned
I wouldn't ever choose to feel this way, these were the
cards I was dealt
My only wish is that more people would understand
how we felt
Sometimes a glimpse of wonder wanders on over
But it's as rare as finding a four-leaf clover
Monsters don't live under our beds
They scream inside of our heads
Still, I live with hope that I will one day win
I will defeat the monster that's under my skin

One Last Letter

If I had the chance to look into your eyes one more
time tonight, I wonder if I'd tell you the damaged
you've caused or if I'd tell you I was doing alright,
maybe if you knew what you had done, just maybe
you'd understand, but I knew that was only a lie as you
could never comprehend what you stole from me that
day, how I was never the same from that moment on,
the memory will never be gone no matter how
desperately I hope it will be erased, I'd wake up and not
be able to recall that look on your face, yet every time I
close my eyes I swear I can see you still, the image
sends a chill down my spine, like a road sign telling me
to turn the other way, there was nothing but darkness
up ahead, and after all of these years I still dread every
moment that reminds me of you, every sight, every
smell, every taste, every noise, walking through my
personal hell, yet I remained poise in each step, not
knowing where the cliff will begin, but I can't go back so
I keep moving forward, only to peer over my shoulder
to see if you're still following, borrowing my innocence
as a shield of your transgression, and as for me; I
remain with one single question...
Do you look at yourself with the same hatred I feel
each time I see my reflection? The shame is an
infection that spreads to every inch of my soul, and the
only part of my body that tells me "it wasn't my fault"
is the circle of my eyes, portraying a deep sorrow

hidden by the disguise of emerald green, I often
wonder if you know what I mean, if you feel guilt so
heavily that some days it takes every ounce of strength
you have to lift your head high, if you play that day over
in your mind like your favourite movie to justify your
choice, if the mention of my name makes your heart
skip a beat or a few, if only you knew what I went
through beyond that one point in time, how it has
changed the way I see the world, the way I see others,
and the way I see myself, how do you look at yourself
knowing you've caused me such great pain, oh that's
right, you don't know, you can't see your chain wrapped
around my wrist, as though it doesn't exist at all, if only
that were true, maybe then my memories of you would
return to the boy with the black wavy hair and a side
smile, the one that drew pictures of dragons on his
homework, imagining a world where you could be
something else was a fantasy I also dreamed, it
seemed as though we had nothing in common, yet we
had a mutual understanding of being unknown, lost in
the crowd of classmates, all the while feeling so alone.
At least we had each other, until even that connection
to security was no more, the door that leads to you will
always be opened, as the heartache can never be
closed, my trust disposed into a lifetime of trauma,
although I hadn't known to define it as such, instead I
buried the feeling of your touch on my skin, I thought
I'd forgotten but I'm reminded that you'll always win,
and you don't even accept your trophy, not knowing the
stakes of the game that you've played, the exchange
we made as I began to slowly fade from reality,

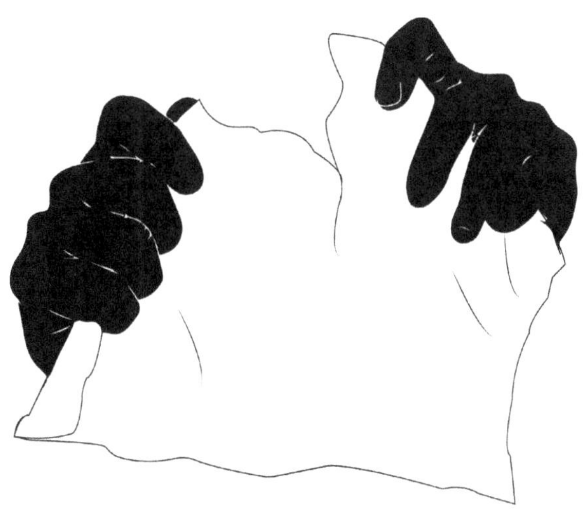

yet they say that I can be free not only from the destruction left in your wake, but free from this internal eternal ache that resides in the center of my emptiness, the fear that my whole world could shake if only I'd allow myself to accept what happened when I was 13, stuck somewhere between a little girl and one on her way to adulthood, and there you stood at the halfway point to make sure I hadn't left unscathed, well congratulations, you've engraved distrust upon my heart, a reason to push away my future friends, or anyone else who only wanted to love me, what does love mean? What does love mean? I wish someone would clarify, because I keep asking myself why I'd love someone only for them to die, or leave, or cause me more pain than I needed, I pleaded with you to like me even after you deemed me broken.

But I guess it's true that actions speak louder than
words, and your actions had spoken, so clearly they
rang in my ears, yet I was absent from tears and for so
many years I thought maybe we could go back to how
we were as kids, clearly I missed the point that you
were no longer that boy I once knew, and admired, and
sure you had your flaws, as do we all, but there was
something about your demeanor that inspired me to
live as I was and not who they wanted me to be, to not
care what other's would think, you were sad, I could
see, maybe even angry, maybe a part of me thought I
could fix it, maybe I recognized it because it was a
mirror to my own disposition, I was sent on my a rescue
mission to help someone who never wanted to be
saved, I was enslaved by my desire to put you back
together,I couldn't help my father, his soul sewn like
leather, but maybe I thought if I could reach the boy
with the black wavy hair and sad eyes, maybe this
lifeboat wouldn't capsize and we could float away from
those who never saw us for who we really were,
doubting what we held inside, at least I tried, but my
efforts were conducted in vain, your name means noise
or loud clatter, as every good memory will shatter like
diamonds in the ruff, that's that we were after all, a
source of untapped potential, the emergence of our
stories was only consequential, and now that's all you'll
ever be.
Another story contributing to every part of me that
people still can't understand, every part of me that I
hate, let's smile for one last school picture day, falsely
thinking the world can only get better, listen closely as I
write the ending to this one last letter, the thought that
you could have done this to another is my own personal

ghost, in fact, this is the truth that still hurts me the
most, plagued by silence; thinking it wasn't as bad as I
imagined it to be, that in some way, at some point,
maybe I'd agreed, that no one would believe especially
after all this time, so I cling to this letter, knowing it as
words you may never read, knowing it may only cause
this wound to bleed more than before, but if these
words could replace the silence of another voice, it is a
choice I'd never choose otherwise, so I'll leave you all
with this one piece of advice: speak, for there is power
in your tongue, it does not matter if you are old or if
you are young, the pain will be released tied to each
word, and you'll be at peace knowing you were heard,
you might not be able to alter the days of prior, but the
future is free for you to acquire, forgive yourself for
something that was not your fault, you, just like me,
can survive sexual assault.

Broken Path

Two roads each facing a different way,
One consisting of rocks and the other sand;
Spreading their lessons across this fair land
Don't gaze down the risky road, though I may
Right and wrong was never for me to say
Once my choice is made, I will grasp your hand
Only to hope that you would understand
It is now that I must choose to go or stay
I take a step toward my awaiting aisle,
This answer does not require a smile
I never wished upon a star to leave
The road in which I go, I must believe
Up into the air with all of my wrath
Forgive me for exploring the broken path

As Far As I Can See

Peering out across the motionless water
No sounds to be heard for miles away
Nonetheless I remain quiet for now
Along with noises of the beautiful bay

Peace surrounds these mountains
Like they've known each other for years
Rekindled spirits together again
The point where the landscape clears

This part of the world so tender
A sacred tombstone set in its place
Somewhere left untouched by us
Like a precious guitar in its case

The view gives off a feeling of glee
And it doesn't stop as far as I can see

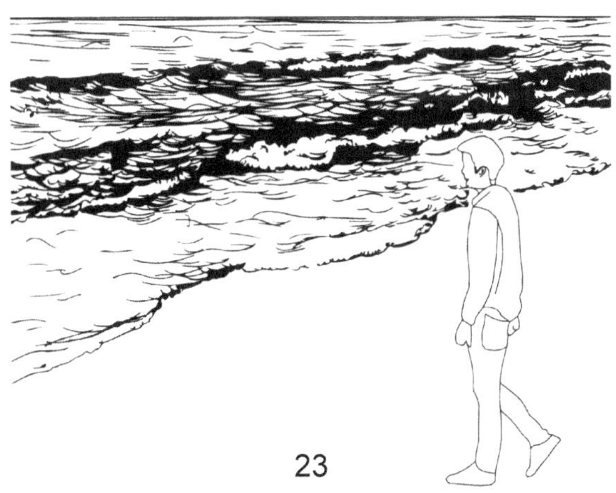

Tip Toe

Shall I dare to take that first step or not
For if I do I may fall or fly
As hidden as the happiness I sought
I get lost in the sparkle of my eye
Sometimes the staircase looks a bit scary
Although you wish the distance could be trimmed
Heavenly peak will be oh so glary
No part of you will want it to be dimmed
The journey will be troublesome and harsh
But those are the challenges that we face
Sometimes you will sink as deep as a marsh
Other times you will rise as high as space
We tip-toe along as far as we see
So that one day we all can, ...will be free

Merry Go Round

Honesty is just a label we put on our words
To make you believe it can't get any worse
Kindness is all of the little things we do
But actions don't always make words true
Braveness is a character we try to play
It merely shows in the darkest of days
Intelligence is all but a worthy tool
It gets you so far til you run out of fuel
Optimism is the most confusing without a doubt
Trying to live life knowing that time will run out
Creativity flows within who we are
Everyone deserves to be the shining star
Forgiveness might be the cruelest sign of fate
Although being forgiven can never come too late
The words that determine who we become
They yell at us until we succumb
In these phrases mistakes are inevitably found
Consistently stuck on a merry-go-round
Caring is a glimpse of what could be
I guess you could say that it's the key
Patience to some can be an everlasting war
Sometimes we forget what we're fighting for
Change is a push in the direction we must go
Around and around until it starts to slow

Tragedy is a reminder that feelings run so deep
Don't ever forget the pain this life will keep
Freedom is proud to ly the leader of this place
It will accept its duties with a sense of grace
Faith is the reason behind life as a whole
It pumps through our mind, heart and soul
Hope, a deceiving weapon that we hold close
It can be there for us when we need it most
Love is strong and bountiful as they claim
It's the picture inside the broken frame
Wisdom wished it met us earlier on
The storm must prevail before the dawn
Peace is when we say "away with the sound"
And we finally step off this merry-go-round

The Way

Two roads pointing in each direction
And only one could my feet follow
As I stood at the intersection
I was brought to introspection
Reflecting upon a soul-aged hollow

The left spoke loudly claiming my regard
While the right remained a mystery
Forward was filled with gates that were barred
Behind me, a distant land that was scarred
One that kept little hope and much history

No choice could I make with confidence
Ticking of the clock rang in my ear
A direction once stole my innocence
Another is met with ambivalence
The latter gives way to a certain fear

'Til I heard a voice, well-known
Like a child in a crowd of noise
That somehow hears her father on the phone
That single voice tells her she's not alone
This is the way, for the other destroys

Revision

If this paper could speak, I wonder what it would say. I've placed the contents of my mind here so many times, this is where they like to stay. It's almost as if the paper understands by now, like we made a vow to listen to each other for eternity, but my turn is approaching me and I can't seem to hear you over the crying, not my tears of course, it's the little girl trying to escape her captor but she's stuck in this chapter and I've been reluctant to continue writing, fighting for inspiration while she inhales her last breath. Since then, I've written many stories, attempting to forget her death but her voice clings to me like a spirit searching for a home, a permanent abode, one that's sewed into the strings of my heart and no matter how far I run, I can never part from her presence.

It's her presence indeed, that yearns to remain; not the memories and not the pain. A constant indication of lament, a citation carved in cement, one that cannot be forgotten or erased, the little girl lives in that hollow place. She never ages, her death lives on, she speaks to me so clearly, it's hard to accept that she's gone.

Trembling in trauma as she stops at the sea
ahead, enemies behind her, the ones she thought
she'd fled, how could she make it to the other side,
the landscape was vast and there was nowhere to
hide, why had she come this far just to be
overtaken, standing alone, yet you said she'd
never be forsaken, fear arose as it had planned
from the beginning.

As she looked back at the fast-approaching
demise, dark clouds permeated throughout the
skies, the sea stared at her in peace and pity, you
may be wondering how it could be both, but you
didn't see its intensity, the girl looked directly into
its smouldering grin, water it seemed but fire
steamed from its very core, and in her distress,
she screamed that she couldn't progress anymore.

The road behind her leads to destruction, the path
in front, needs no further introduction, she
became acquainted with the sea all too well, but
similar to a well it appeared without a bottom, the
limits to its bounty were undeniable, yet woefully
reliable, she didn't know what this meant but she
knew that if she could only get through, her
journey would be complete, she'd finally be freed
from those chasing her every mile, maybe then
she'd learn how to smile, maybe then she could lie
at the feet of the one who has walked beside her
all along, maybe then she could move on from the

memories that haunt her each day and each night, so she grabbed the only thing she had left, the only thing she carried, and began to write.

Maybe your voice enters the ears of all, the minds of most, and the fingers of few. This note may be her last but she thanks you for speaking through her hands that are frayed, the ones that clasped the blade, yet the same hands that prayed in desperation, like the heart cry of a nation pleading for your presence, if only our trust was without transience, but she wrote to you in anonymity, knowing you'd be the only one to read her final words, like the birds in the sky she wished she could fly beyond and most of all she wished that you'd respond before it was too late…

"Put down the pencil and carry your cross, I won't lift you up and take you across with my able hand, but I promise you that your feet will rekindle their love with the land, you will not be swept away by waves that overwhelm, instead you will know the way of thy heavenly realm, but I caution you before you take a stride, to remember how far you have come, not to forget that you could have died, it is not because of anything you've done, every tear you've cried has created this great sea, but as I wipe them away, this I shall decree: when you flee from your enemy and your feet embrace the ground, take a deep breath and look around, this

is not where you once were nor where you'll reside
ever again, I've redeemed you from bondage and
broken every chain, when your hope was little and
hard was your heart, I knew that I had called you
from the very start, I desire not to have watched
you in such despair, but believe me when I tell you
'there was no moment, I was not there', you might
not have seen the promise I foretold, because I
wanted you to have something you could hold, so
kneel down and choose your very stone, as
evidence of the seeds that I've sewn, I will be
faithful to guide you from where you now are, but
never forget who has brought you this far"

As the waves became a great wall, she was
reminded of it all. The pain she'd spoken and that
left unsaid, the night she almost entered the
community of the dead, the blockage of truth that
her conscious refuses to reveal, everything that
you have yet to heal and everything you've already
mended, all of the seas that have already ended,
and she didn't realize that the sea was red by the
blood you shed because every time she bled you
protected her from the permanent scar, simply
because of who you are and the love that you
share.

She searched her entire life for the promised land,
only to discover that she had been there, since the
day you spoke to her fingertips, while you could

have sent all the ships on earth and one boat, that day she learned that you were all she needed to stay afloat. That little girl walked on solid soil, distant from fear, the battle was finished and all her enemies could hear, it was no longer the echoing of her weeping, but the sound of victory seeping into every crevasse made by those who sought to bring her down, only you wouldn't allow her to drown, your plan was much greater than anyone could envision, she may have thought her story was written, but God was working on a revision, that no one could stop reading.

Case Closed

I walked into a courtroom filled with people I didn't
recognize
And I thought to myself; would this be the day of my
demise?
For there was no reason to argue or deny the claim
As Satan held a file that was stamped with my name

All of the sins that held me captive over the years
Evidence of my betrayal echoed into my ears
I knew what I had done and where it would lead
My life was filled with my lies, deceit and greed

Yet when I tried to present a defense for my trial
I felt I was already walking the green mile
No hope was left in this barren spirit of mine
A placement the judge would surely assign

I couldn't plead my innocence and prove them right
Although I couldn't leave this world without a fight
The jury was amused at my attempt to explain
Maybe my efforts were conducted in vain

In a frantic search for mercy I fell on my knees
But the demons had spoken with incredible ease
Just as I was about to accept my conviction
A man rushed in and freed me from affliction

His face was unfamiliar but the jury was afraid
When He looked at me, I knew my debt was paid
I told the stranger that I was so glad He came
And He whispered "for you I will take the blame"

Handcuffs wrapped around the wrists of this man
I hadn't known that it was all part of the plan
Down the hall and past the cell, we went
There was no time left for me to repent

Why were they taking Him away from the jail?
And why would they pierce His skin with a nail?
This sight will be forever trapped in my mind
At that moment, it's like our souls intertwined

How could a stranger come and take my place
He knew who I was but I'd never seen His face
Somehow our bond was greater than I'd known
As deep as the ocean and as strong as a stone

For some reason I didn't view this ending as just
While His body would decay, turning into dust
Then there's me... What was I supposed to do?
Everything I'd witnessed, none of it seemed true

His body was beaten and broken as He bled
After three more days He would rise from the dead
It was then that I'd finally understand my role
That my body was separated from my soul

And Jesus had come to win the battle I lost
As He gave his life for my sin on the cross
Instead of judgment, I was given redemption

Still to the call of the devil, I was no exemption

But He gave me the strength to overcome temptation
As He spoke the good news across the nation
He forgave me for my transgressions and wrongs
So I will worship Him through the chords of songs

Only Now I was given the wisdom to choose
I could retreat to the past or walk in His shoes
I've decided to believe in the words of the Bible
For He promised that our lives would be vital

The climax of the story weaved by his sorrow
No longer afraid of what will come tomorrow
The sacrifice He made could never be repeated
We can't give in to the enemy, He defeated

His love for us is greater than all satisfaction
But this gift can be wasted by our distraction
We mustn't forget this chance we've been granted
Indeed, Jesus placed a seed, in us to be planted

Satan no longer controls His sons and daughters
In the midst of an obstacle, He'll part the waters
We can cry out to him in the truth of a prayer
For He hears each drop of a single tear

He created the future we know nothing about
Our hearts can be healed without a doubt
We can live the way that God had intended
Through Christ, human nature can be amended

The power that is born from his very name
 Will free us from the grip of every chain
When we trust that His hand is upon our shoulder
He'll lock and seal our file in his folder

At last, the past is never to be reviewed
Because of Him, we have been renewed
Because of Him, we have been redeemed
In what seemed, like an unrelenting test
But now, we can rest, for we've been blessed
We Thank Him for saving us from this bondage of guilt
Forever rejoicing in the life that He has built

I Will Survive

When I'm reminded of my past mistakes
Weighed down by its heavy guilt
When you condemn me for all that I've done
I'll show you all that I've built

When I mark the wall with my growth
And you cover it in paint
When I stare at myself in the mirror
As I listen to your complaints

When you bring addiction, sin to my mind
As it slowly permeates
When I'm plagued with thoughts greatly perverse
And they open up black gates

I will survive

When my stomach groans with disappointment
And my head will pound alike
When the mountain seems too immense to climb
That's when I begin my hike

When I observe what thy hands hath made
In its bounty and splendor
When I undergo each of the seasons
I bow and thank the sender

When I grow weary, tending to my wounds
Yet they continue to bleed
When His blood mixed with mine touches soil
'Til harvest births from a seed

I will survive

When I ponder your flawless reputation
One that can stand on its own
When I read of your worthy character
And how you died all alone

When I understood your love paid the price
On the cross that fatal day
When I see how you have proven yourself
I promise you, I'll stay

When I begin to explore the valley
And the fog occludes my route
When I search for the road behind me
And all that I find is doubt

I will survive

When I think I've learned all there is to know
My prayers only imitations
When I've lost my passion for things you do
And I neglect your nations

When complacency becomes my response
'Tis your mercy that I'll seek
When overwhelmed by the cares of this world
'Tis your voice that must speak

When my ears ring and my eyes are blinded
Unaware of when you're near
When I mistake strength as my possession
Remind me that you are here

So, I will survive

When the books of history are final
and my name cannot be found
When we have overstayed our welcome
Upon this fertile ground

When my feet arrive at the finish line
And my race has now ended
When I meet you face to face, you'll say
I lived how you intended

When you arrive, asking for your people
On a cloud in all your glory
When you come to find me and take my hand
And close the book to my story

I will survive
Only then, will I survive

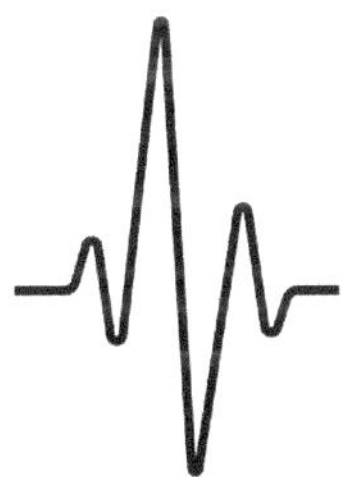

To Forgive You

To forgive you after all I have known
Not to be forgotten but raised anew
'Tis as the scrapping of my skin from bone
So shall be my separation from you
Delicate with all sensitivity
One slight motion causing permanent pain
Like a surgeon's precise activity
An accuracy that is hard to maintain
Your fingerprints embedded in my skin
Your words forever speaking to my heart
And these memories that exist within
I await the day that they shall depart
To forgive you is a display of love
Thus, unforgiveness is the lack thereof

Presence

Your presence surrounds me again
Greater than a drug touching my veins
Greater than all the world could gain
And when I realize you are near
The days of deep sorrow and pain
They, too, tremble in holy fear

One moment, when I touch your hand
When I finally seek your face
Tears roll from my eyes and arms expand
As I'm engulfed in your embrace
If it pleases you to do so,
May you make me your dwelling place

Won't you come, let your spirit flow
I await its divine descent
When you come, this truth that I know
Will arrive without argument
Before you, I shall bow my face low
For there is glory, when you're present

There is glory in your presence

Without You

45

The voice in my head is all that I can hear
Telling me "don't forget to take a breath"
Only I think I'd rather just disappear
And shake hands with the host of death

I was beaten by someone I didn't expect
And then I faded away into the air
It's safe to say that my flesh was wrecked
The worst part is that I didn't even care

You see, my life was consumed by trials
Which is why I am here in the first place
I have walked in these shoes for miles
To find the purpose that I could embrace

Somewhere along the way I lost my hope
And my destination seemed unclear
I began using sin as a way to cope
enabling it to take the wheel and steer

The untimely death struck me at midnight
While the rest of the world was fast asleep
Pain consumed me like a luminous light
But soon, the darkness would begin to creep

The earth fell from beneath my weary soul
As my heart was stolen from my chest
The sky changed to red, the ground into coal
And I pray you never witness the rest

I pleaded my case but no words would form
And he had no ears upon his scared head
Suddenly the others, like flies would swarm
For a moment, fear told me I wasn't dead

My body had never felt quite so weak
As I tried to fight the other inmates
But there was no mercy that I could seek
Only wide walls with no exits or gates

I was speechless to the horror that I saw
I desperately wanted to cry or scream
It was then that I heard the teeth gnaw
And I assumed that this must be a dream

I had never seen a day as dark as the one now
This may not be true when tomorrow arrives
I wished for answers that this world wouldn't allow
A world with a foundation made out of knives

A lifetime of mistakes flashed before me
It was too late to change the flow of time
Upon the ashes, I bowed down on my knee
To face the punishment for my crime

I'm sorry to the family that I failed
And the friends that I always pushed away
I took for granted each breath that I inhaled
Now my only wish is that I could stay

I'm sorry for the sins in which I depended
If only I'd known the fate that awaited me
I was blind until my world had ended
Finally the truth opened my eyes to see

Show me the wrong direction that I turned
For I will not make that same mistake twice
Take me to a time where I could have learned
And provide me with eternal advice

My wish may be lost in this place of despair
Echoing forever in the tomb of hell
But I'll lift my request up to you in prayer
For a final chance at the story I will tell

My hands are clean and my legs are walking
Hadn't my destiny already come?
My eyes are open and my lips are talking
And yet my body no longer feels numb

My flesh was burned in the heat of the flame
While my soul met with a stranger I knew
I hadn't known the extent of my shame
Until he was able to change my view

He showed me the piece that I had lost
The reason why I lived a life of woe
Because Jesus had already paid the cost
So that you and I would be allowed to grow

He loved me more than any sin by human hand
Or any mistakes that I could have made
More than any object or piece of land
Or an amount of money I could have paid

I was ignorant to the words in your book
Deaf to the songs that would praise your name
Now that you've caught me with your mighty hook
No way my life will ever be the same

For strength will now run its course through my
veins
And joy will penetrate my peaceful heart
Only you Lord, can break all of the chains
While granting the sinner a brand new start

There's no enemy that I should have to fear
As you are always walking by my side
You know every need and you wipe every tear
There's no reason for anyone to hide

I can place all my trust in the unseen
As I believe in the promise you gave
Don't need to look where I've already been
To know that I am no longer a slave

You've constructed a purpose for me alone
One that I can not fulfill without aid
For I can accomplish nothing on my own
Evident in the times that I have strayed

Without you, the world was a scary place
Not knowing if today would be my last
Without you, There's no smile on my face
Constantly hiding behind a mask
Without you, I was lost in a sea of pain
That I could not stand to bare much longer
Without you, the devil would call my name
But now I've become so much stronger

Without you, I aimlessly wandered the earth
Lonely but afraid of trusting another
Without you, I couldn't see what I was worth
Reflected in the eyes of a mother

Without you, I stood on the edge of destruction
And saw a future I didn't desire
Without you, I went back to the introduction
Until you came and lifted me higher

Without you, I was a broken vinyl
Repeating the sorrow that I created
Without you, my fallen fate was final
I'm so glad that you patiently waited

To Be Loved By You

How might I praise thee? Oh, mine holy God
For praise is to love, and love without restrain
The type of love that one cannot explain
Your mercy speaks when my voice is weary
You still forgive me, even though I'm flawed
Even though I stumble and though I fall
You whisper to remind me of my call
And you don't perform so we will applaud
That's just who you are, your kindness revealed
Though time races by, you never change
You remain the same, mystery concealed
This gift you've given shan't be a waste
To place this pen in my hand as I yield
For your love is the finest I'll ever taste
And your love oh God, forever my shield

Grain of Sand

Take this thought upon thy mind!
And, in parting you shall find,
The secret of mankind —
T'was wise to have wondered
How our days are numbered;
Yet, misguided in a way
In a night, or in a day,
All we have known could be gone,
And it won't be very long
T'il all we can see
Are the tracks of the enemy

I stand amid the crowd
Declaring my faith aloud,
And I hold within my hand
A single grain of sand —
A reminder, I keep
In my mind while I'm asleep,
While I weep — while I weep!
O God! Can you not save
Before they're in the grave?
Like sand, a single soul
Oh God! Won't you make them whole?
You died so I'd be free
But you didn't die only, for me

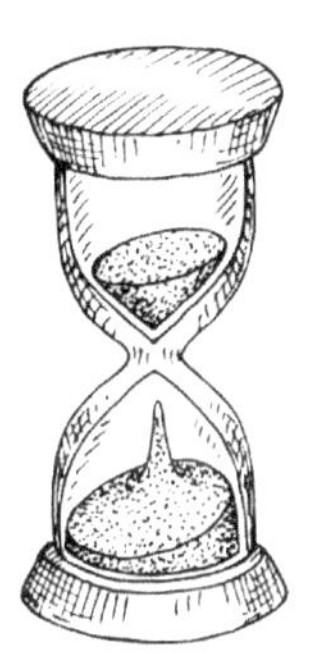

Mission of Mine

Once again, I became re-acquainted with the setting I knew too well, surrounded by the voices that told me I wasn't brave enough to end my suffering. But as I spoke those words to you in a moment of vulnerability, you told me, that the cowardly pull the trigger while the courageous choose life. Desperately I wanted to believe the words leaving your lips, but my teeter-totter tips towards negativity, towards doubt, towards shame, if I thought I could survive, I'd hide in that place of self-blame, for just a little longer… but how much longer?

There comes a time when I have to realize that this world waits for no one, that it keeps spinning whether I'm on the ride or I fell off years ago. Like the kid that won't stop pushing the merry-go-round even when you say that you're feeling sick, so you either endure until it stops or you take the leap, risking greater pain. I know it's not the same but imagining these images of a childhood untainted by reality makes it easier to explain. If you knew the train in my mind at this time, you'd understand why I'd want to begin with something more polite.

Because the battle I now fight, makes me forget simple memories like this. The smile of innocence, the fearlessness of a child as she jumps into the water to swim, as she climbs trees and swings on ropes, she licks her ice cream as though it's the last time she'll taste something so sweet and runs her fingers through the fur of a dog like it's the first time she's ever felt fabric so soft, she'll look up at her parents dreaming of the day when she'll be just like them, so successful; so happy, so kind, but that's where the mind fools me. You see, all of these pleasantries are mere examples of everything that was stolen, everything that was lost, everything that fades further into the frost that consumes me each day. I warned you that I wouldn't have many nice things left to say.

Maybe what I described earlier carefully correlates with the memories of your past, but those are the last things I'd use to tell of my former life. I barely recall myself as a child and if I thought it was possible, I'd argue that I was never that young, never that innocent, never so naïve to believe that this world was not entirely disguised by light. The darkness is everywhere, if only you'd allow yourself to focus on what's in front of you instead of being allured by temporary satisfaction, it's a distraction that has caused many to function in a trance.

A fatal dance where life is the lead and
with each step you bleed more and more
until the floor is cherry red and there is
nothing left but a skeleton of who you
once were, the line between that little girl
and this corpse begins to blur in a maze of
confusion, you fall deeper into the
delusion that breathing equals living, but
so many are living today and so few are
alive. We can strive for perfection, God
knows I've tried, but in this election, death
is tied to the majority, the dissection of the
shield that once wrapped itself around us
has forsaken us and taken our authority.

When did we become so feeble? So frail?
That we bought into this sale of our souls,
when did we begin to walk in ignorance,
indifferent to deliverance? Am I the only
one who sees the true color of gray that
closes in around us like the walls of a
prison cell, was my former life completely
washed from my memory, am I already in
hell? I can't tell. I wish someone would tell
me. Someone who could see what I see. But
they all assume I'm crazy and continue to walk in
unison towards their destruction. They emphasize
more efficient production while being enticed by

the seduction of this world, each one led astray by
a single handshake with death. I've been trying to
warn you but I'm running out of breath.
I've also been a victim strapped on this conveyer
belt, I've known your struggle, I know how it felt to
be helpless, awaiting your demise, but as I
go around and around I can't seem to close
my eyes, I just watch you all complacent
and composed, defenseless and exposed,
I've searched for the controls, dreaming of
the day I'd find the switch to stop this
motion, but the longer I swirl in the midst
of this commotion, the further I am from
experiencing emotion.

While passionate to save you, I'm
inexplicably numb. These words may not
reach you, but I hope you know why I've
come. Not to overturn my inevitable fate,
but to trust that I'm not too late to show
others the truth, even if only a few so I
wouldn't be out here alone, if only I'd
known the complication of my call, it's as
though I'm staring at a mountain begging
it to fall, to crumble into the pieces of the land I
now reside, how am I supposed to guide you
through the rubble? To protect you from
impending trouble that is bound to arise with
force, I'm filled with remorse but at least I'm no

longer empty, I have plenty of darkness to provide
the illusion that the hole inside of me is no longer
vacant, just be patient, that's what I tell myself,
but it seems as though the clock ticks faster each
time I make a mistake, this ache, similar to that of
a merry-go-round, never leaves my core.
I don't know how much longer I can engage in war
with weaponry, the discrepancy between my
worth and my mission, between what I
deserve, and my current condition of
inadequacy, I use that word casually but it
fuels the mechanics that keep us trapped
in this cycle, unable to slow down, unable
to stop, was I placed here as punishment?
To listen but not hear, to watch but not see,
to touch but not feel. To be given the
knowledge of this place, the display in a
glass case, the empathy that forces me to
relate, but not the ability to create a better
outcome, instead I am given the vision of
your decomposition over time, the
impossible mission of mine, plagued with a
burden I can no longer bare, with the truth that
my tongue refuses to share, clothed with layers of
heated despair, transparent in the costume I wear,
given one role to help you live not relying only on
air, armed with the barren words of a hollow
prayer. This task was one never meant for
someone as insignificant as me, the little girl was

abandoned on the playground because no one
came to take her home, home; the place where
one lives permanently, that place existed
somewhere she was never meant to be.

Alabaster Box

A great cost, even greater sacrifice
A life dedicated to you, alone
Poured out at your feet, each personal vice
Believing in the power of your throne
T'is all that I had left, this decision
The one thing I clenched tightly in my grip
T'was eternity that I'd envision
The hope that if I let go, you'd equip
Afraid this work was heavier than I
But more afraid of not working at all
I remember the night I looked at the sky
And I promised that I'd accept the call
My alabaster box broken before you
These words spilt on the pages of breakthrough

www.ingramcontent.com/pod-product-compliance
Lightning Source LLC
LaVergne TN
LVHW021235200726
843509LV00012B/1500